Milet Picture Dictionary

English·Spanish

Milet Publishing Ltd
PO Box 2459
Chicago, IL 60690
USA

Email info@milet.com
Website www.milet.com

First published by Milet Publishing Ltd in 2003

Text © Sedat Turhan 2003
Illustrations © Sally Hagin 2003
© Milet Publishing, LLC 2010

ISBN 9781840595130

Printed and bound in China by 1010 Printing International Ltd, May 2010.

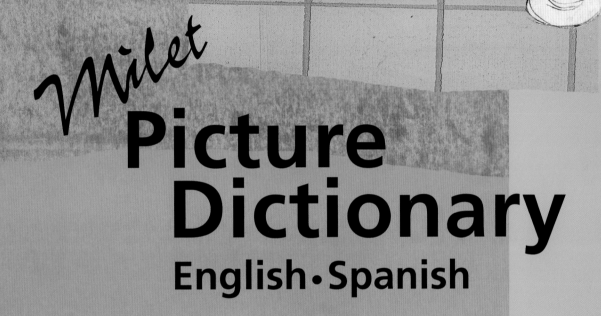

Milet Picture Dictionary
English·Spanish

Text by **Sedat Turhan**

Illustrations by **Sally Hagin**

COLOURS/COLORS
COLORES

red
rojo

orange
naranja

yellow
amarillo

green
verde

blue
azul

purple
púrpura

grey
gris

pink
rosa

black
negro

white
blanco

PLANTS
PLANTAS

tree
árbol

orchid
orquídea

rose
rosa

sunflower
girasol

daisy
margarita

tulip
tulipán

grass
césped

lily
azucena

daffodil
narciso

branch
rama

leaf
hoja

cactus
cactus

watering can
regadera

plant pot
tiesto

FRUIT
FRUTA

cherry
cereza

kiwi
kiwi

apricot
albaricoque

pear
pera

fig
higo

peach
melocotón

strawberry
fresa

banana
plátano

mango
mango

orange
naranja

apple
manzana

blueberry
arándano

lemon
limón

grapes
uvas

avocado
aguacate

raspberry
frambuesa

grapefruit
pomelo

pineapple
piña

ANIMALS
ANIMALES

zebra
cebra

lion
león

tiger
tigre

giraffe
jirafa

elephant
elefante

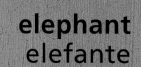

polar bear
oso polar

penguin
pingüino

duck
pato

cow
vaca

rooster
gallo

sheep
oveja

goat
cabra

horse
caballo

ANIMALS & INSECTS
ANIMALES E INSECTOS

bird
pájaro

dog
perro

cat
gato

rabbit
conejo

frog
rana

crab
cangrejo

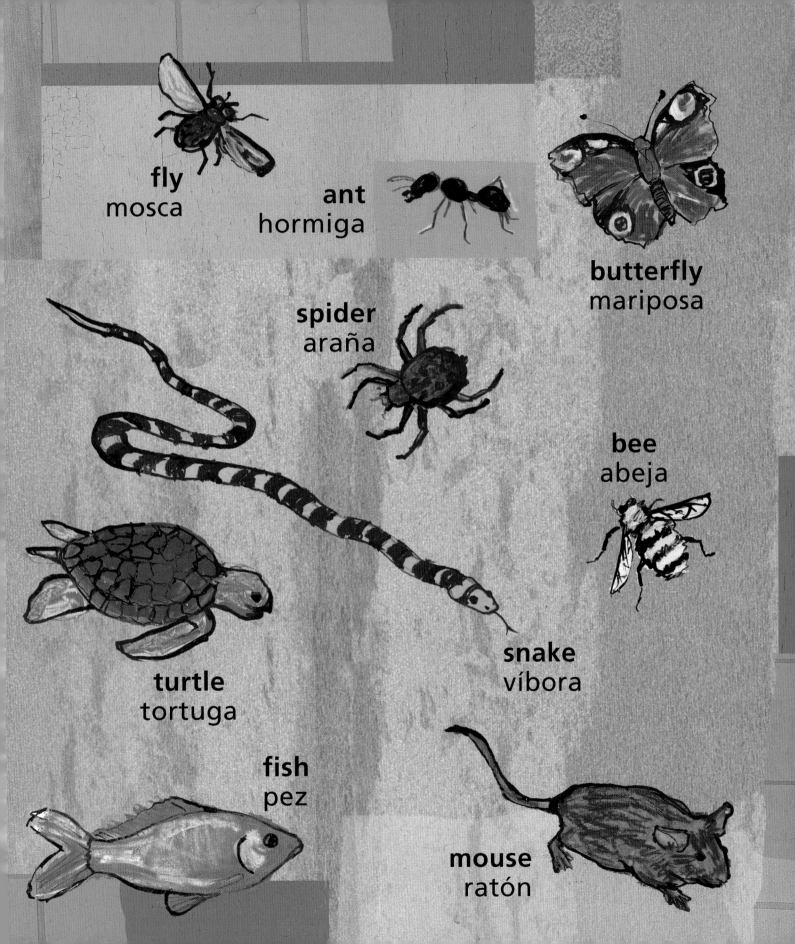

fly
mosca

ant
hormiga

butterfly
mariposa

spider
araña

bee
abeja

turtle
tortuga

snake
víbora

fish
pez

mouse
ratón

HUMAN BODY
CUERPO HUMANO

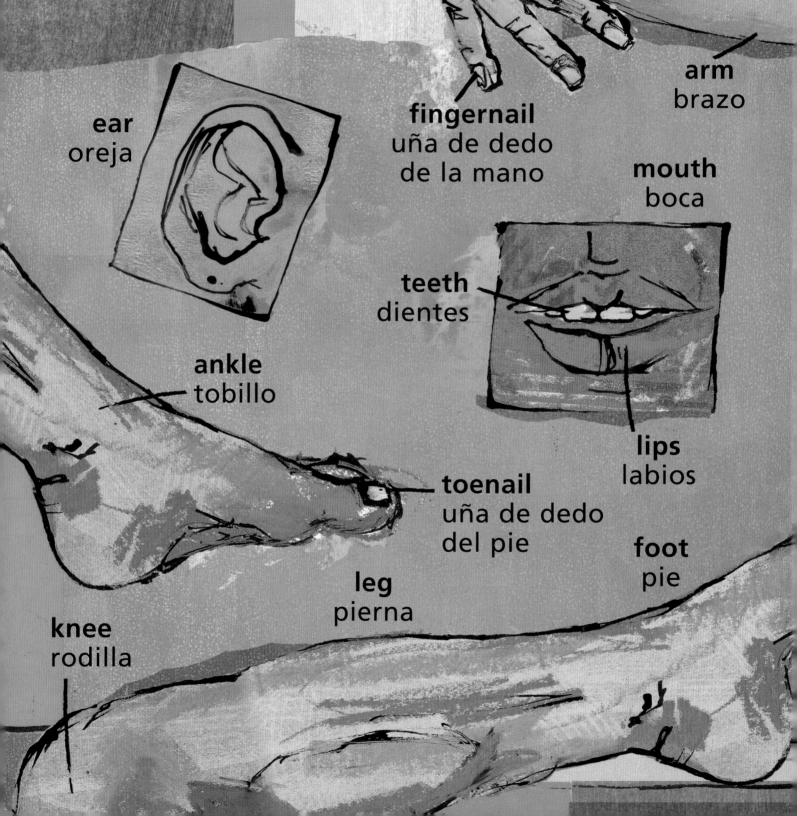

ear
oreja

fingernail
uña de dedo
de la mano

arm
brazo

mouth
boca

teeth
dientes

ankle
tobillo

lips
labios

toenail
uña de dedo
del pie

foot
pie

leg
pierna

knee
rodilla

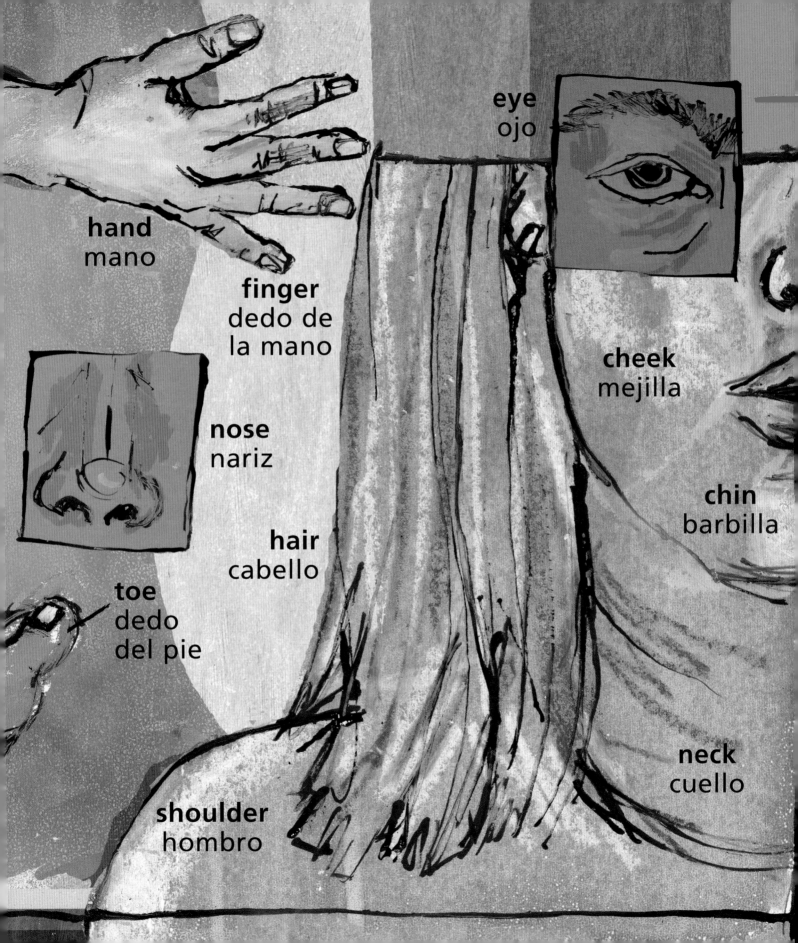

hand
mano

finger
dedo de
la mano

nose
nariz

hair
cabello

toe
dedo
del pie

shoulder
hombro

eye
ojo

cheek
mejilla

chin
barbilla

neck
cuello

HOUSE & LIVING ROOM
CASA Y SALA

house
casa

chimney
chimenea

roof
tejado

door
puerta

armchair
sillón

key
llave

candle
vela

light bulb
bombilla

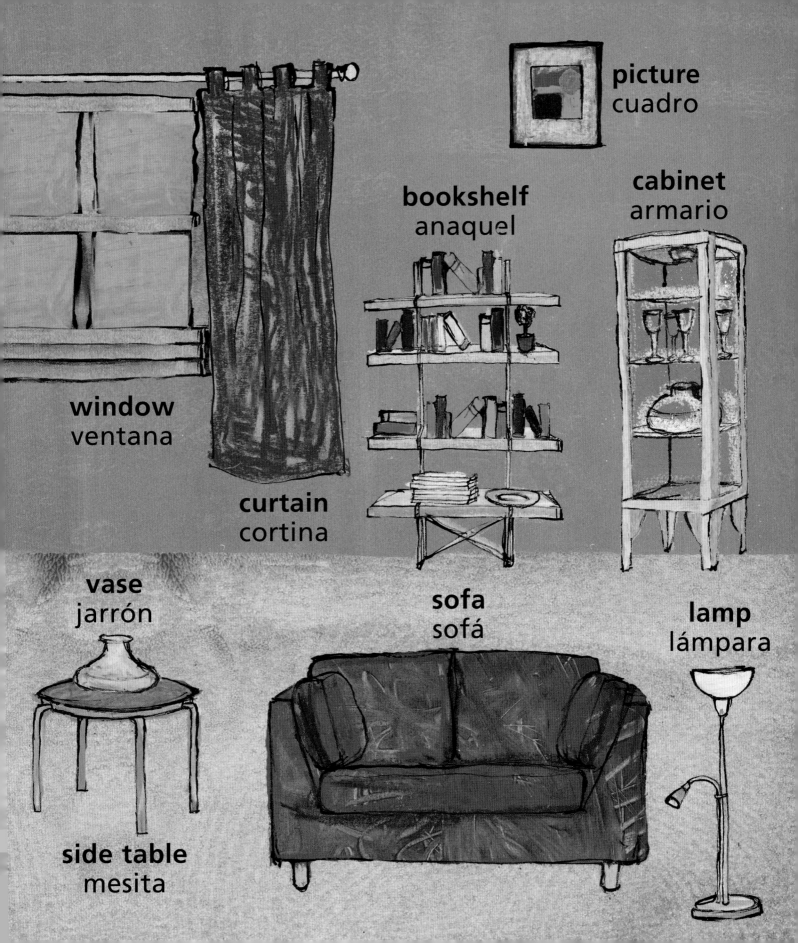

picture
cuadro

bookshelf
anaquel

cabinet
armario

window
ventana

curtain
cortina

vase
jarrón

sofa
sofá

lamp
lámpara

side table
mesita

KITCHEN
COCINA

bowl
cuenco

glass
vaso

refrigerator
nevera

plate
plato

napkin
servilleta

teapot
tetera

cup
taza

table
mesa

chair
silla

spoon
cuchara

knife
cuchillo

fork
tenedor

frying pan
sartén

saucepan
cacerola

oven mitt
guante para
el horno

dishcloth
paño

toaster
tostadora

stove
cocina

sink
fregadero

oven
horno

VEGETABLES
LEGUMBRES

potato
patata

green bean
judía verde

mushroom
seta

carrot
zanahoria

asparagus
espárrago

onion
cebolla

pumpkin
calabaza

peas
guisantes

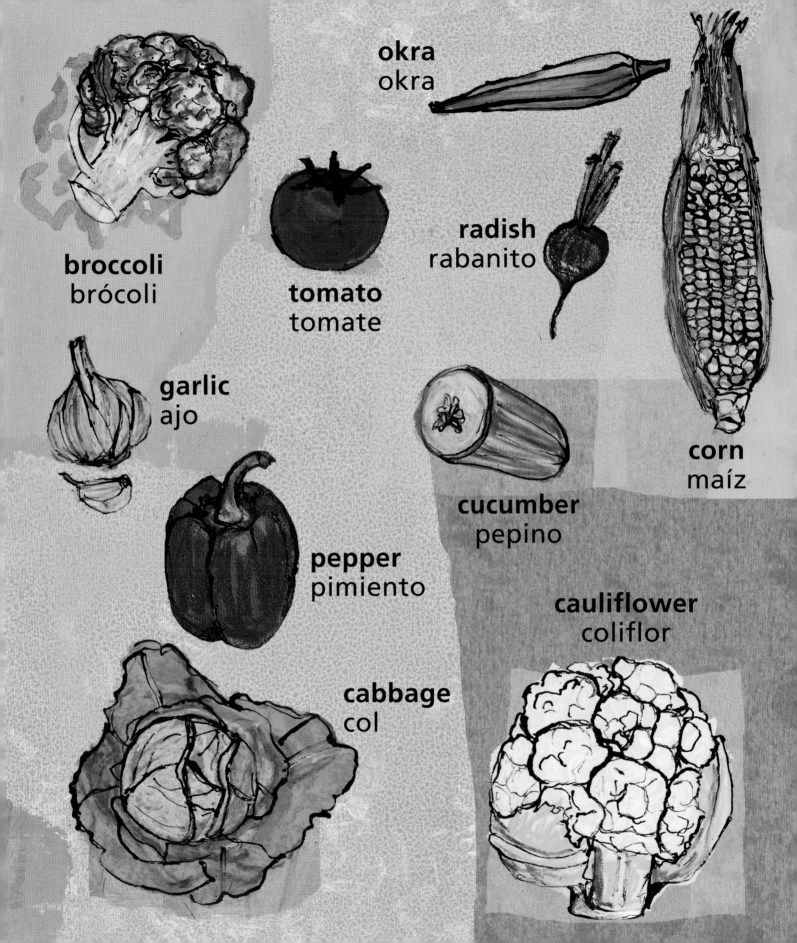

okra
okra

broccoli
brócoli

tomato
tomate

radish
rabanito

corn
maíz

garlic
ajo

cucumber
pepino

pepper
pimiento

cauliflower
coliflor

cabbage
col

FOOD
ALIMENTOS

sandwich
emparedado

bread
pan

cheese
queso

milk
leche

butter
mantequilla

jam
mermelada

honey
miel

egg
huevo

cereal
cereal

raisins
pasas

oil
aceite

fries
patatas
fritas

fruit juice
zumo de fruta

spaghetti
espaguetis

chocolate
chocolate

cake
pastel

ice cream
helado

BATHROOM
CUARTO DE BAÑO

mirror
espejo

towel
toalla

sink
lavabo

toilet paper
papel higiénico

toilet
inodoro

bathroom cabinet
armario del cuarto
de baño

potty
orinal

hairbrush
cepillo

hairdryer
secador

shower
ducha

comb
peine

toothpaste
pasta dentífrica

shampoo
champú

conditioner
acondicionador

toothbrush
cepillo de dientes

soap
jabón

bathtub
bañera

BEDROOM
DORMITORIO

bed
cama

alarm clock
despertador

bedside table
mesita de noche

hanger
percha

rug
alfombrilla

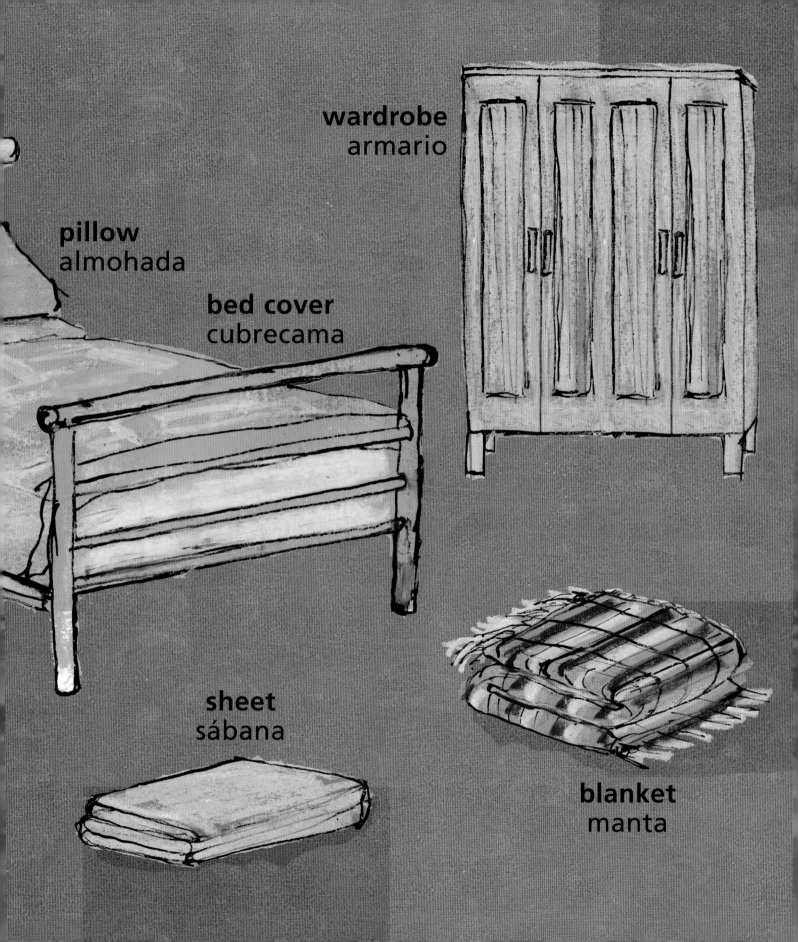

wardrobe
armario

pillow
almohada

bed cover
cubrecama

sheet
sábana

blanket
manta

CLOTHING
ROPA

gloves
guantes

umbrella
paraguas

button
botón

glasses
gafas

boxer shorts
calzoncillos

T-shirt
camiseta

underpants
calzoncillos

hat
sombrero

sweater
jersey

jacket
chaqueta

slippers
zapatillas

scarf
bufanda

backpack
mochila

skirt
falda

shirt
camisa

handbag
bolso

socks
calcetines

belt
cinturón

jeans
vaqueros

pyjamas
pijama

shoes
zapatos

shorts
shorts

COMMUNICATIONS
COMUNICACIONES

telephone
teléfono

television
televisor

DVD player
reproductor de DVD

video recorder
grabador de vídeo

remote control
control remoto

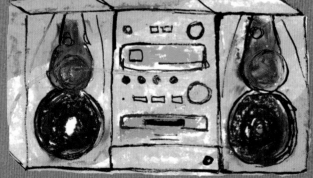

stereo
estéreo

video camera
videocámara

camera
cámara

TOOLS
HERRAMIENTAS

screwdriver
destornillador

screw
tornillo

saw
serrucho

stepladder
escalera

nail
clavo

drill
taladro
eléctrico

hammer
martillo

shovel
pala

vacuum cleaner
aspiradora

paint
pintura

SCHOOL & OFFICE
ESCUELA Y OFICINA

pencil
lápiz

glue stick
pegamento

marker
rotulador

book
libro

stamp
sello

ruler
regla

pencil sharpener
sacapuntas

pencil case
estuche

crayon
lápiz de color

scissors
tijera

globe
globo terráqueo

stapler
grapadora

tape
cinta adhesiva

calculator
calculadora

paints
pinturas

paintbrush
pincel

pen
lapicera

envelope
sobre

computer
ordenador

desk
mesa

notebook
libreta

NUMBERS
NÚMEROS

one
uno

two
dos

three
tres

four
cuatro

five
cinco

six
seis

seven
siete

eight
ocho

nine
nueve

ten
diez

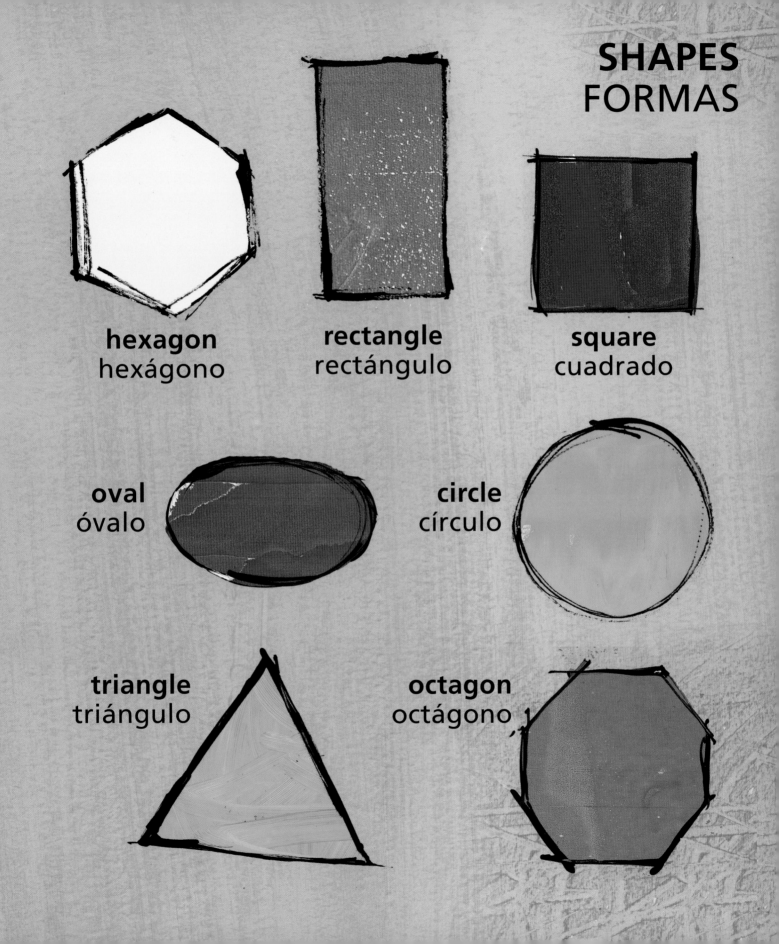

SHAPES
FORMAS

hexagon
hexágono

rectangle
rectángulo

square
cuadrado

oval
óvalo

circle
círculo

triangle
triángulo

octagon
octágono

MUSICAL INSTRUMENTS
INSTRUMENTOS MUSICALES

flute
flauta

guitar
guitarra

violin
violín

saxophone
saxofón

bongos
bongos

clarinet
clarinete

drums
batería

trumpet
trompeta

piano
piano

xylophone
xilofón

SPORTS & GAMES
DEPORTES Y JUEGOS

skateboard
monopatín

video games
videojuegos

cards
naipes

**football /
soccer ball**
balón de
fútbol

ice skates
patines de
cuchilla

rollerblades
patines en línea /
rollerblades

skis
esquíes

chess
ajedrez

baseball
béisbol

basketball
baloncesto

glove
guante

bat
bate

American football
fútbol americano

tennis ball
pelota de tenis

tennis racket
raqueta de tenis

cricket ball
pelota de críquet

cricket bat
bate de críquet

TRANSPORTATION
TRANSPORTE

boat
barco

bicycle
bicicleta

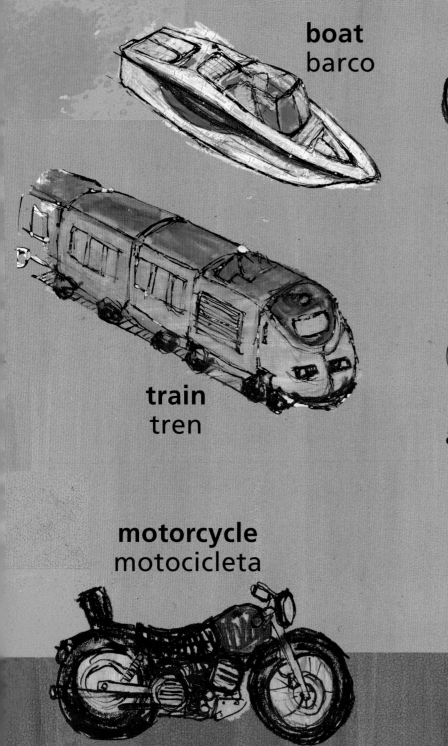

train
tren

car
automóvil

motorcycle
motocicleta

ambulance
ambulancia

helicopter
helicóptero

plane
avión

fire engine
coche de bomberos

bus
autobús

truck
camión

tractor
tractor

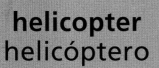

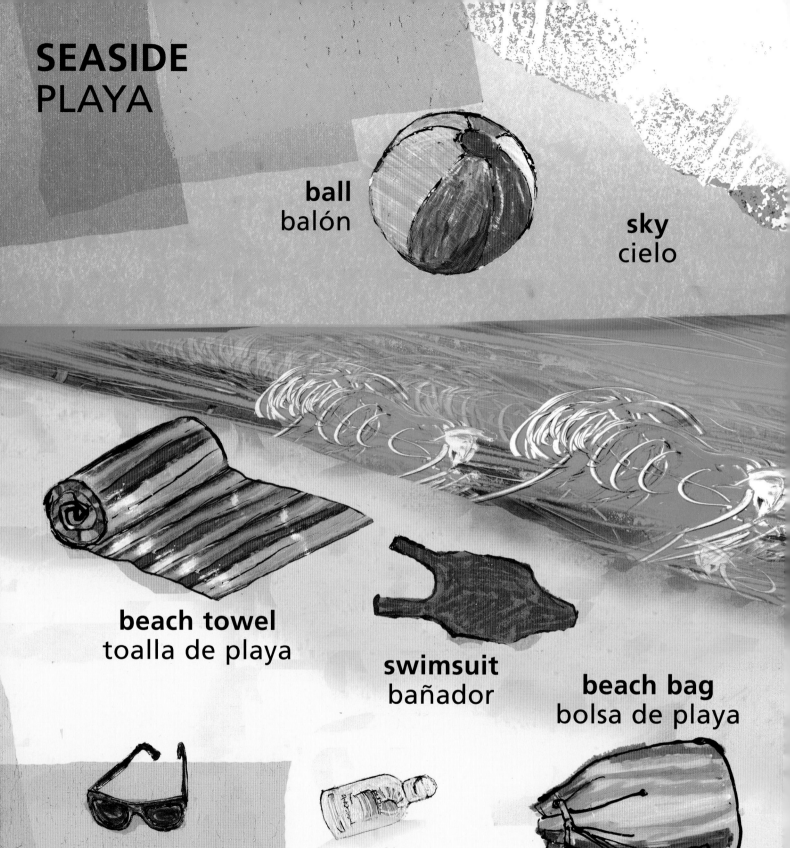

SEASIDE
PLAYA

ball
balón

sky
cielo

beach towel
toalla de playa

swimsuit
bañador

beach bag
bolsa de playa

sunglasses
gafas de sol

sunscreen
filtro solar

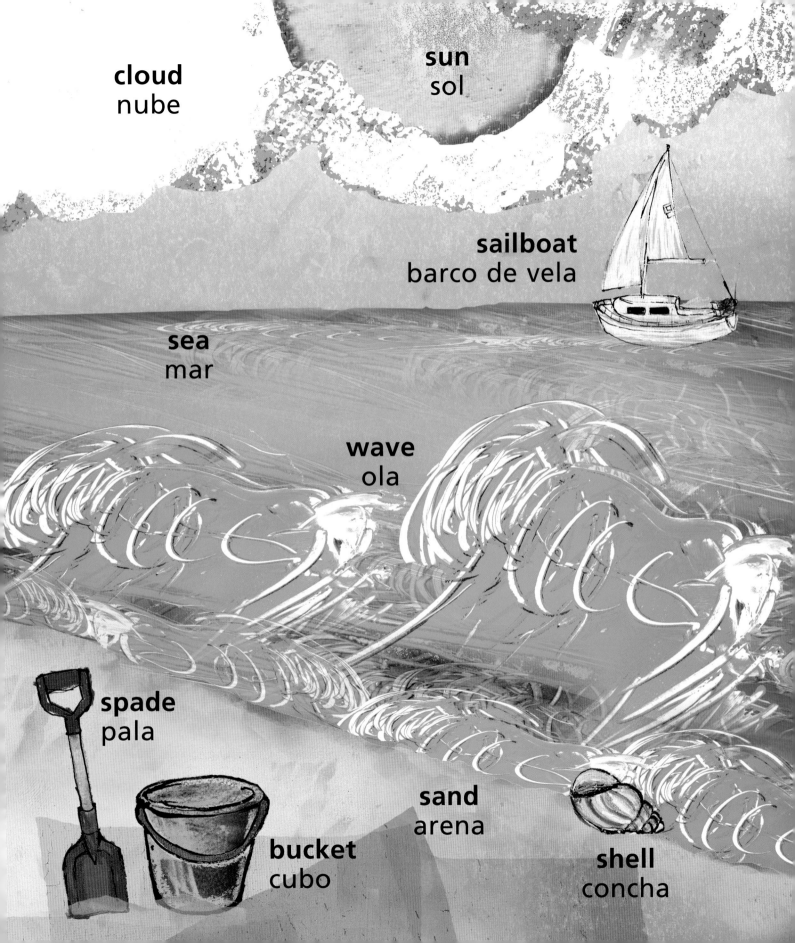

cloud
nube

sun
sol

sailboat
barco de vela

sea
mar

wave
ola

spade
pala

bucket
cubo

sand
arena

shell
concha